BIOLOGY Field Notes

Be a HIPPO Expert

by
Alex Hall

Minneapolis, Minnesota

Credits
All images are courtesy of Shutterstock.com, unless otherwise specified. With thanks to Getty Images, Thinkstock Photo, Adobe Stock, and iStockphoto.

Recurring – LadadikArt, Milano M, The_Pixel, yana shypova, vectorplus, Macrovector, NotionPic, Shotvideo. Character throughout – NotionPic. Cover – vectorplus, Ihor Bondarenko, Nils Versemann, Shotvideo, Vilmos Varga, Milano M, The_Pixel, Macrovector. 4–5 – Radek Borovka, Henk Bogaard. 6–7 – Ondrej Prosicky, schusterbauer.com, Vineg, pandemin. 8–9 – Ralph Lear, FCG. 10–11 – Eleseus, Ondrej Prosicky. 12–13 – Lena Ivanova, Alexander Hilber. 14–15 – nwdph, Nick Greaves. 16–17 – BigBoom, Mogens Trolle. 18–19 – Kaitlind Fasburg, Steve Barze, Scotch. 20–21 – Jens Goos, Fayad Hameed. 22–23 – Tomas Drahos, sasha_gerasimov.

Bearport Publishing Company Product Development Team
Publisher: Jen Jenson; Director of Product Development: Spencer Brinker; Managing Editor: Allison Juda; Editor: Cole Nelson; Associate Editor: Naomi Reich; Associate Editor: Tiana Tran; Designer: Kim Jones; Designer: Kayla Eggert; Designer: Steve Scheluchin; Production Specialist: Owen Hamlin

Library of Congress Cataloging-in-Publication Data is available at www.loc.gov or upon request from the publisher.

ISBN: 979-8-89577-005-4 (hardcover)
ISBN: 979-8-89577-436-6 (paperback)
ISBN: 979-8-89577-122-8 (ebook)

© 2026 BookLife Publishing
This edition is published by arrangement with BookLife Publishing.

North American adaptations © 2026 Bearport Publishing Company. All rights reserved. No part of this publication may be reproduced in whole or in part, stored in any retrieval system, or transmitted in any form or by any means, electronic, mechanical, photocopying, recording, or otherwise, without written permission from the publisher. Bearport Publishing is a division of FlutterBee Education Group.

For more information, write to Bearport Publishing, 5357 Penn Avenue South, Minneapolis, MN 55419.

CONTENTS

Meet the Biologist............4
A Hippo's Body...............6
River Homes..................10
Splashing Around 12
Dinner Time..................14
Watery Leftovers 16
Family Life..................18
Life Cycle...................20
Hilarious Hippos 22
Glossary.....................24
Index 24

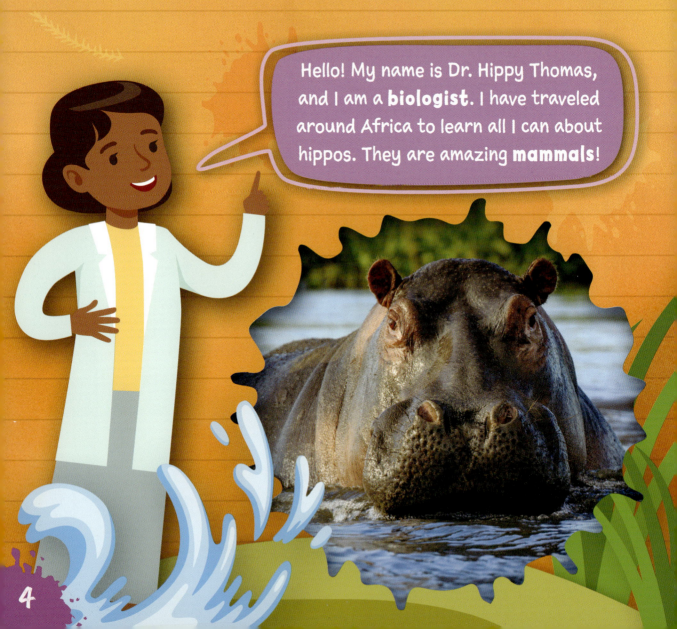

Being a hippo **expert** is a lot of work. I filled this notebook with everything I know about hippos. Will you read it? Together, we can find out even more!

A HIPPO'S BODY

Hippos are large animals with smooth, thick skin. Being under the hot sun can make their skin dry. So, hippos let out an oily, red **substance** from their bodies to protect themselves.

Red oil on a hippo's skin

Some people used to think the red oil was blood.

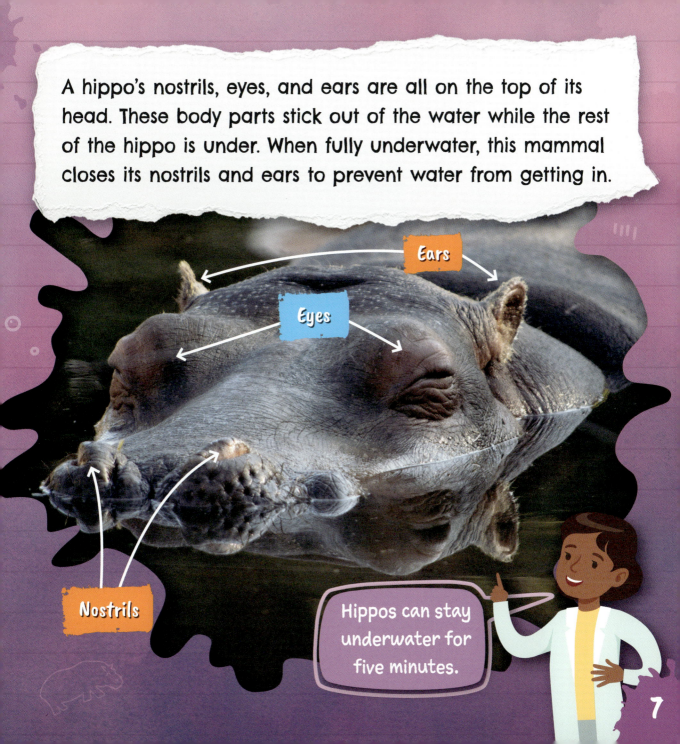

A hippo's nostrils, eyes, and ears are all on the top of its head. These body parts stick out of the water while the rest of the hippo is under. When fully underwater, this mammal closes its nostrils and ears to prevent water from getting in.

Ears

Eyes

Nostrils

Hippos can stay underwater for five minutes.

Hippos are known as **aggressive** animals. When other creatures get too close, hippos may open their mouths and show off their long, sharp teeth. They use their huge teeth to scare or fight with other animals.

Hippos have four different kinds of teeth.

Hoof

Hippos are the third-largest mammals on land.

Hippos have webbed toes, which means their toes next to each other are joined by skin. Hippo toes are also covered with hooves. These large, strong nails protect the toes.

RIVER HOMES

The name *hippopotamus* is an old Greek word that means river horse. The animals got their name because hippos are usually found near freshwater habitats, such as slow-moving rivers and lakes, in sub-Saharan Africa.

A habitat is the place where a plant or animal lives.

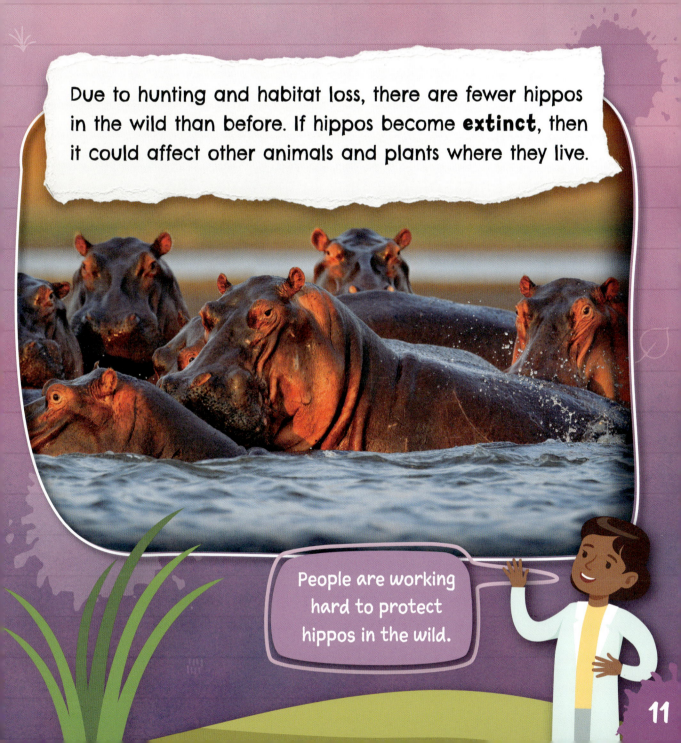

Due to hunting and habitat loss, there are fewer hippos in the wild than before. If hippos become **extinct**, then it could affect other animals and plants where they live.

People are working hard to protect hippos in the wild.

SPLASHING AROUND

Hippos spend most of their time in the water. This helps them stay cool in the heat. However, hippos cannot actually swim. Instead, they go to the bottom and push themselves along the river floor.

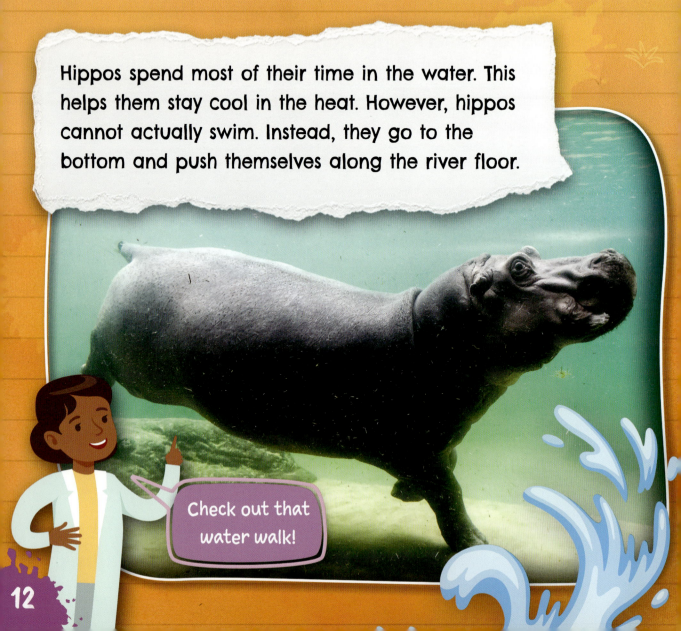

Check out that water walk!

During the day, hippos often take underwater naps. They bob up to take a breath and sink back down again . . . all while staying asleep!

Hippos are too heavy to float.

DINNER TIME

Hippos are herbivores, which means they eat plants. Hippos eat mostly short patches of grass that grow near water. These grassy areas are sometimes called hippo lawns.

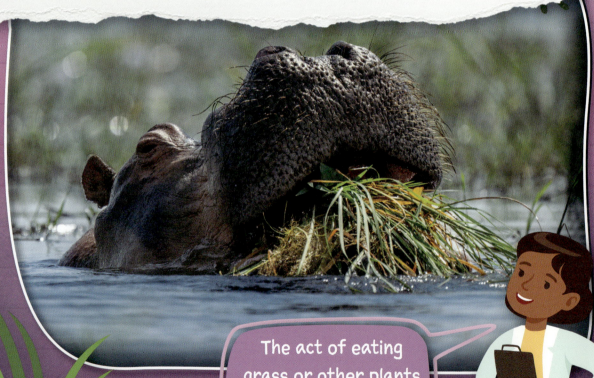

The act of eating grass or other plants is called grazing.

WATERY LEFTOVERS

All that food has to come out sometime! Hippos often poop in the water. Their dung is actually full of useful leftovers. Over time, these bits mix into the water to keep rivers and lakes healthy for other animals.

Many fish feed on the hippo dung left behind.

Hippos also use poop to mark their area. They do this by spinning their flat tails around while dropping their dung. The smell keeps away hippos that are not part of their group.

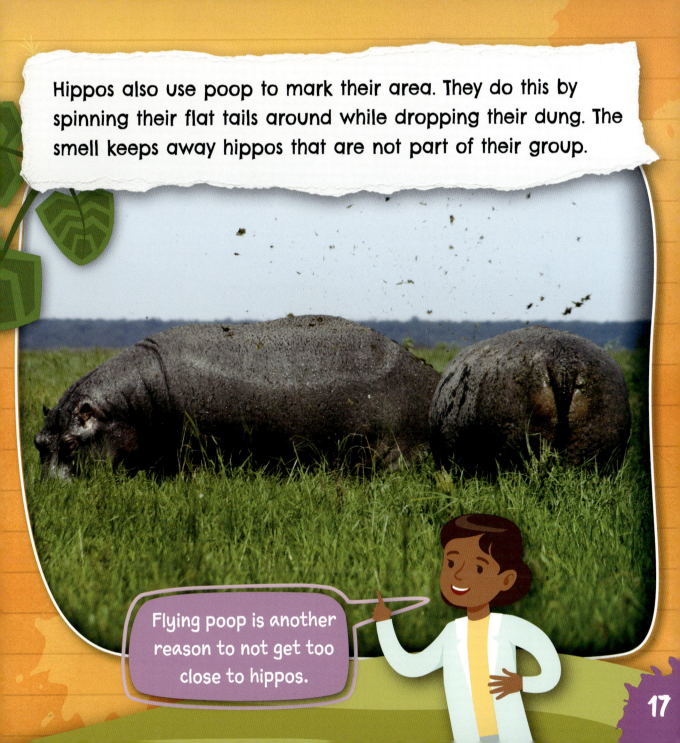

Flying poop is another reason to not get too close to hippos.

17

FAMILY LIFE

Hippos live in groups called herds or pods. There are often between 10 and 40 hippos in a herd. However, some herds can have up to 200 animals.

A hippo's honk can be as loud as a car horn!

These mammals **communicate** with one another through snorts, grumbles, and wheezes. Hippos can make a special noise that sounds like a wheeze honk. It is so loud that it can be heard from almost 1 mile (1.6 km) away!

LIFE CYCLE

A life cycle includes the different stages of an animal's life.

Hippo life cycles start with babies called calves. Every two years, **female** hippos leave the herd to give birth to one calf each. Soon, the mothers return to the herd with their young.

There can be several **male** hippos in a herd, but only one is **dominant**. This male is the protective leader of the group. If this leader sees danger, he will aggressively splash and show his sharp teeth.

Hippos can live for about 40 years in the wild.

HILARIOUS HIPPOS

From napping underwater to creating poop whirlwinds, hippos are hilarious creatures! I hope you've enjoyed learning about these amazing mammals.

You have just begun your hippo adventure. There is so much more to learn about them. Continue to study. Soon, you'll be an expert, too!

GLOSSARY

aggressive likely to attack

biologist a person who studies and knows a lot about living things

communicate to share information

dominant the most powerful or the strongest

expert a person who knows a lot about something

extinct when a kind of plant or animal has died out completely

female a hippo that can give birth

male a hippo that cannot give birth

mammals animals that are warm-blooded, drink milk from their mothers when they are young, and have fur

substance the material something is made of

INDEX

Africa 4, 10
blood 6
grass 14–15
herds 18, 20–21

lakes 10, 15
nostrils 7
poop 16–17, 22
rivers 10, 12

skin 6, 9
teeth 8, 21
toes 9
water 7, 12, 14–16